M.O.B.
Cooking
– MY OWN BLEND –

Written by BeBe's Daughter

M.O.B. Cooking: My Own Blend

Copyright © 2021 Cheryl Manzi

Produced and printed by Stillwater River Publications.
All rights reserved. Written and produced in the
United States of America. This book may not be reproduced
or sold in any form without the expressed, written
permission of the author(s) and publisher.

Visit our website at
www.StillwaterPress.com
for more information.

First Stillwater River Publications Edition

ISBN: 978-1-955123-33-4

Library of Congress Control Number: 2021914310

1 2 3 4 5 6 7 8 9 10
Written by Cheryl Manzi
Published by Stillwater River Publications,
Pawtucket, RI, USA.

Publisher's Cataloging-In-Publication Data
(Prepared by The Donohue Group, Inc.)

Names: Manzi, Cheryl, author.
Title: M.O.B. cooking : my own blend /
written by BeBe's daughter, [Cheryl Manzi].
Other Titles: MOB cooking
Description: First Stillwater River Publications edition. |
Pawtucket, RI, USA : Stillwater River Publications, [2021]
Identifiers: ISBN 9781955123334
Subjects: LCSH: Cooking, Italian. | LCGFT: Cookbooks.
Classification: LCC TX723 .M36 2021 | DDC 641.5945--dc23

*The views and opinions expressed
in this book are solely those of the author(s)
and do not necessarily reflect the views
and opinions of the publisher.*

M.O.B.
COOKING

My Own Blend

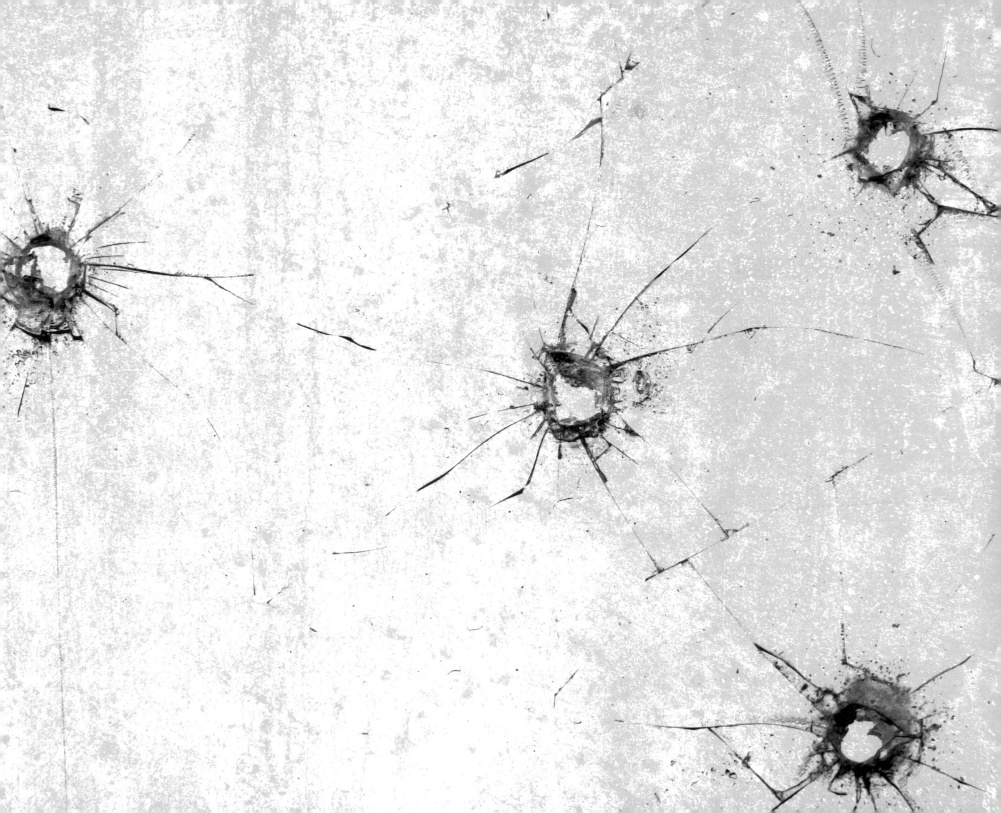

CONTENTS

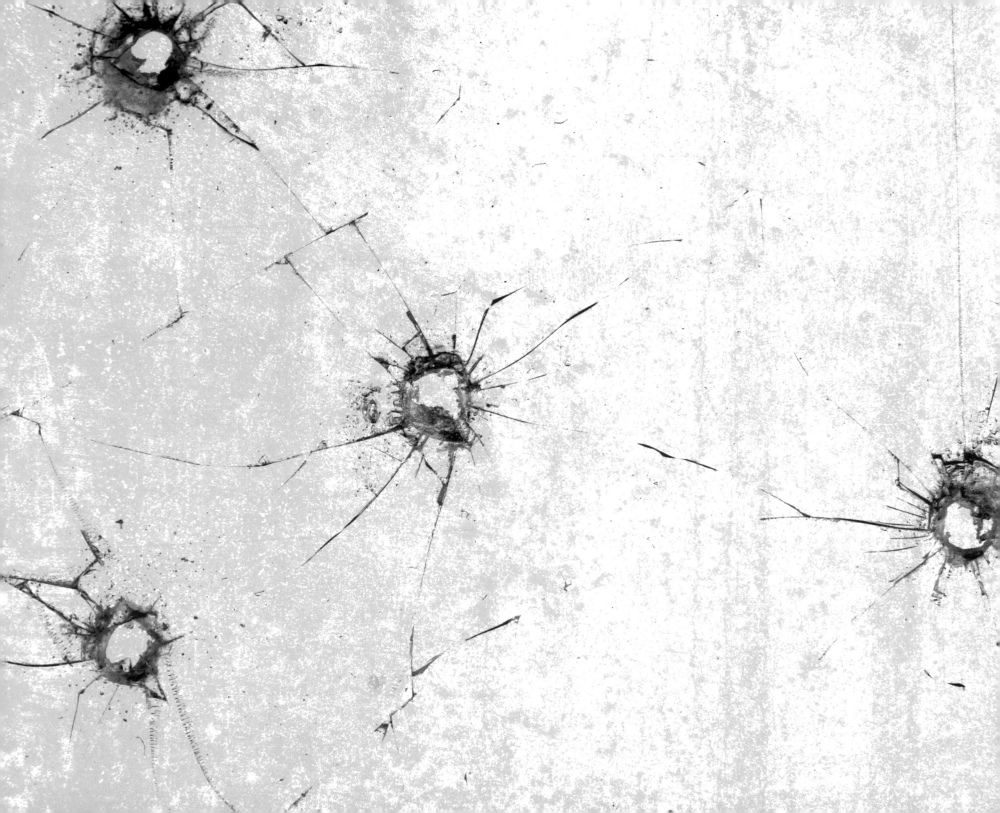

ACKNOWLEDGEMENTS / INTRODUCTION

WHERE WOULD I be without my family? Family are the roots and foundation of who we are and become. I feel blessed for having my grandparents who traveled to this country and brought with them the traditions and love of food from Italy. I am very proud of my Italian heritage, of my mother and father, and of the very large Italian families they both came from. Aunts, uncles, cousins, and friends of the family that were our extended family. My relationship with my grandfather Pasquale Troia, my mother's father, and all the memories that I cherish still to this day of our time spent together. The bond created from family is still with us to this day. Cousins. We do not see each other like we used to back in the day, but the bond is still there. The caring for each other does not go away with the loss of our parents and we do not have those Sunday dinners every week, but we still have our memories and traditions that were passed down to us.

This Italian-American cooking guide has recipes from the kitchen, not from a 5-star restaurant. It has simple food from the heart and little stories that will hopefully put a smile on your face while you are cooking up these dishes!

Thanks to my husband Frank Calcagni, my daughter Cheron, and especially my cousin Pasco for putting up with me and my crazy and wild dreams and adventures that I take them on. And my family and cousins, love you with all my heart.

Onto the next adventure....

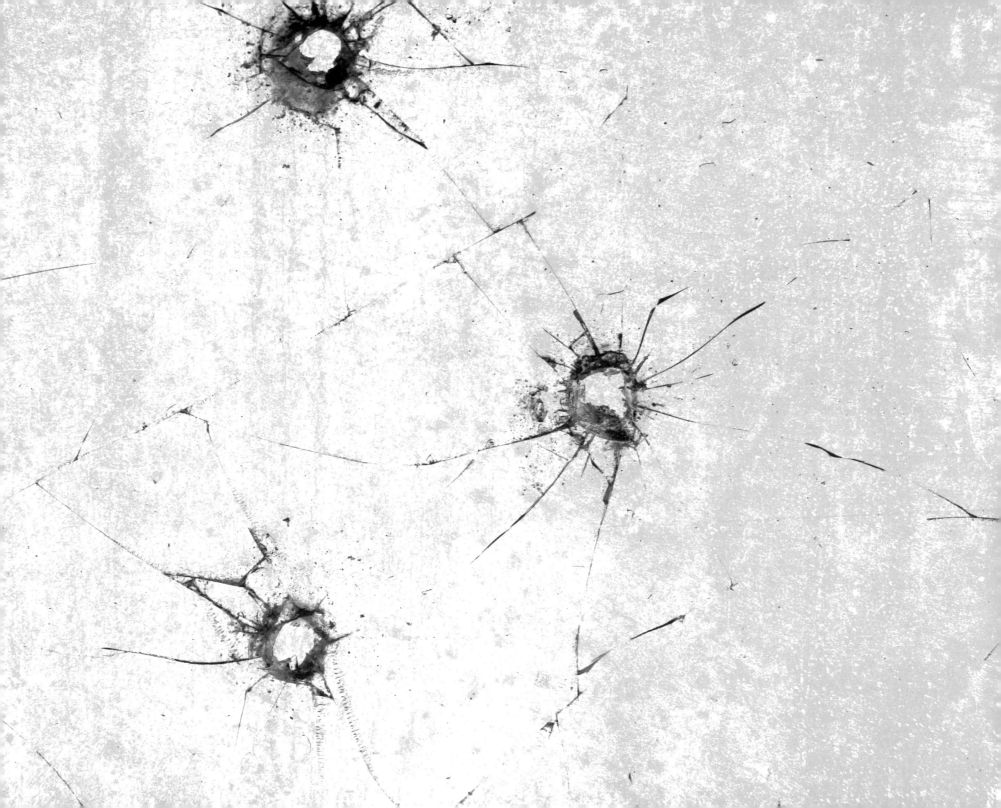

COOKING FOR THE MOB!

THIS IS A cookbook based on Albina's recipes and cooking for the Mob.

These recipes come from the passion Albina had for cooking and any names characters, places, and incidents are either the product of the author's imagination or are used fictitiously. And resemblance to any persons living or dead, businesses, companies, or locals is entirely coincidental.

Just when she wanted out of the kitchen... she was pulled back in!

From a five-year-old's perspective

The year: 1960-something. The place: a three story tenement house in Providence, Rhode Island.

Since I was the last born, the baby of the family, there was a 10 year gap between me and the oldest of three siblings. I spent my time attached to Albina's (nickname: BeBe) apron strings. She couldn't go anywhere without me hanging with her from the small kitchen in our second-floor apartment. From my earliest memories, all I can remember is the food being prepared and cooked daily by Albina. It wasn't until I was an adult and put all the pieces together that I realized my mom was a cook for the Mob!

Short stories follow these great recipes. Some you will find amusing. I just thought this was all normal, and I guess to me, in my world, this was....

BeBe's daughter Cheryl, age 5.

First let me say this is how I remember the characters from the neighborhood

We had

The Bread Man	The Egg Man
The Fish Man	The Vegetable Man
The Milk Man	The Sausage Man

Then we had

Tony C, Little Tony, T, Big Tony, Senior, Junior (first or last names not needed), Jake, Jake the Snake, Jake from the Lake, and a list of Frankies and Johnnys. Not to mention, Slick, Beanzy, The Mouth, Rat, Joey Bananas, and Crazy Eddie.

I believed these were their actual names. What did I know, I was only five.

No one called me by my name. I'm sure they didn't even know it. I was known as BeBe's kid. "She belongs with BeBe," is what they would say.

And then there was the big shiny black car that would pull up to the house and two men would carry bags of food to be prepared up to the second floor and say, "Here BeBe, have this ready for one today!"

Make them a meal they can't refuse!!!

I Know a Guy...

It also seemed that BeBe knew a guy for everything. Pre-mall days, we would shop at Uncle Carlo's—everything from linens, underwear, jeans, Bambi's work clothes, leather jackets, and so on... The basement of Uncle's house was like going to the mall.

As a kid, we never asked any questions... This just seemed like this was the way it was.

When I needed something, BeBe would just say, "Go see your uncle." And it seemed like we had a lot of uncles! They seemed to come and go. My mom would just say, "Uncle will be gone for a while..." I just thought they were on vacation. And when they would come back, BeBe would take them to get new suits and our third-floor apartment seemed to be always ready for that Uncle who was returning... from vacation.

Make them a meal they can't refuse!!!

One thing about Albina's kitchen—it was her way or no way!

There was no, "Oh honey, what would you like for dinner?" She cooked—it was on the table—you ate, you did not refuse!

This was the same no matter who she was cooking for.

Cooking for the guys meant a lot of food too go. Maybe for their road trips to the woods? And it wasn't for hunting…. Anyway, "sangwiches" (sandwiches) was her specialty.

There were always tins in the kitchen filled with egg biscuits and wine biscuits, for that little bit of a sweet taste after any meal.

Make them a meal they can't refuse!!!

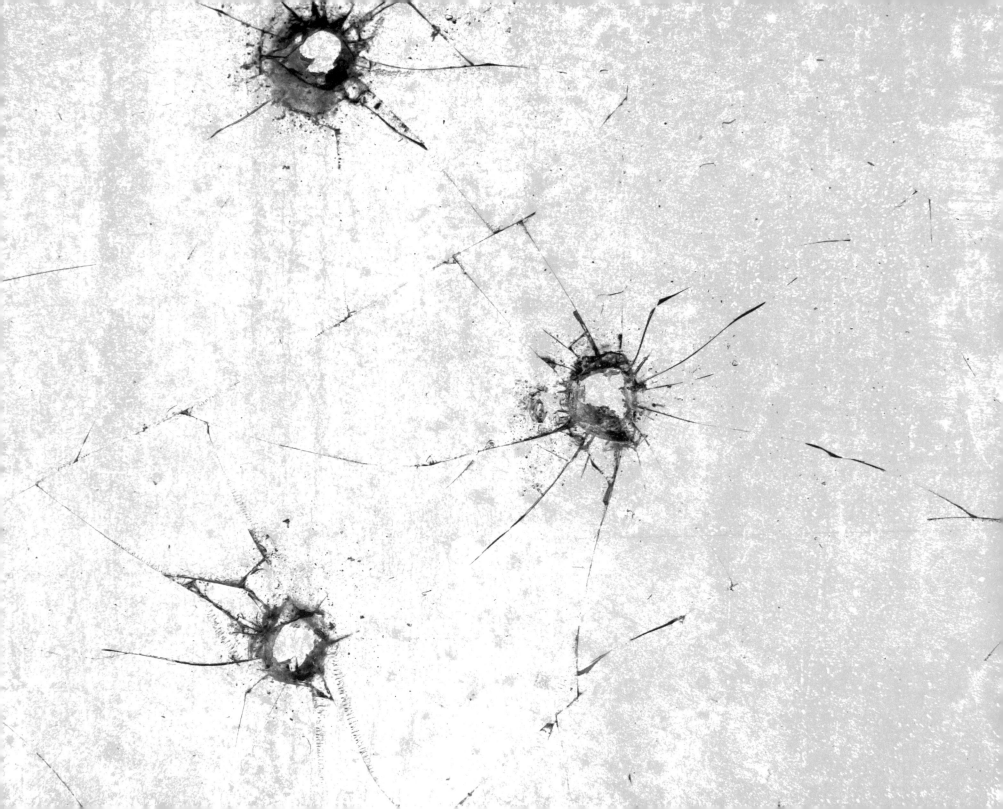

THE CLASSIC ITALIAN GRINDER

INGREDIENTS

¼ pound Genoa salami, thinly sliced
¼ pound Capicola (hot or sweet),
    thinly sliced
¼ pound Prosciutto, thinly sliced
¼ pound ham, thinly sliced
¼ pound Provolone
Grinder/sub rolls

Toppings
Chopped romaine or iceberg lettuce
Sliced tomatoes
Sliced red onion
Sliced pepperoncini
Roasted red peppers
Red wine vinegar
Olive oil
Salt & pepper

Red Wine Vinaigrette
6 crushed garlic cloves
½ cup red wine vinegar
Pinch of red pepper flakes
2 teaspoons Italian seasoning (dried
    Italian herbs)
1 teaspoon salt
¼ teaspoon black pepper
1 cup olive oil

ALBINA WAS KNOWN for her sandwiches to go, so we can't leave out the Italian grinder!

Since Albina did her shopping on Federal Hill, we were lucky to have access to the best authentic Italian grocery stores around. They provided the best meats, cheeses, and fresh bread, which made these sandwiches more than just sandwiches.

Mix the olive oil, vinegar, and seasonings in a Mason jar, shake well, and set aside. Slice the rolls lengthwise, not cutting quite all the way through. Drizzle with the olive oil mixture.

Lay a couple of slices of each meat, followed by the cheese, then another layer of each. Top with the sliced veggies and drizzle with the red wine vinaigrette and a little salt and pepper.

Now that's Italian!

PEPPERS & EGGS SANDWICHES

INGREDIENTS

Olive oil
1 large red pepper
1 large green pepper; cored and
    seeded and cut into 1 inch pieces
8 large eggs (from the egg man)
Salt and pepper to taste
Italian torpedo rolls (from the
    bread man)

Heat oil in skillet over medium heat. Add peppers, salt, and pepper. Stir the peppers often, approximately 15 minutes until browned. Beat eggs in bowl adding a tablespoon of milk or cream, add to pan. Allow eggs to set and stir again.

Now at this point you could flip this frittata by placing a dish over the pan. Pick up the pan and over the sink, flip and slide it back into the pan to finish cooking. (This takes practice.) Or, you could place a cover over the pan until it is finished cooking.

This is a good traveling sandwich you could serve hot or cold, and it stays good wrapped in foil. BeBe used to wrap it in wax paper first, then foil.

POTATOES & EGGS SANDWICHES

INGREDIENTS

3 medium potatoes, peeled
¼ cup olive oil
Salt and pepper to taste
8 large eggs, beaten
1 loaf Italian bread or Italian rolls

Cut the potatoes in half, then slice each half into ¼ inch slices. Heat oil in skillet. Pat potatoes dry and place in skillet. Cook, turning the pieces frequently, until the potatoes are browned and tender, about 10 minutes.
Sprinkle with salt and pepper.

Beat eggs with salt and pepper. Pour the eggs over the potatoes.
When the eggs have begun to set, turn the potato and egg mixture.
Cook, turning the potatoes and eggs occasionally, until the eggs are done to taste.

Cut a lengthwise slit in bread and pull out the soft crumb from the center.
Fill the bread with the potatoes and eggs.
Cut loaf into 4 sandwiches.

SANDWICH STEAKS
(ala Italiano)

INGREDIENTS

8 to 12 thin sandwich steaks,
    flattened
Egg wash (flour / egg /
    breadcrumbs)

Add grated Parmesan cheese to breadcrumbs.

In fry pan, heat oil until hot.
Fry 3 to 4 minutes on each side until golden crisp

Serve in nice Italian rolls topped with gravy (red sauce) and slice of provolone.
Or top with sliced tomato, lettuce, and drizzle with olive oil.

Serve right away, or wrap to go.

SAUSAGE, PEPPERS & ONIONS
(Classic)

INGREDIENTS

2 large green peppers
1 Vidalia onion
2 lbs sweet Italian sausage (from
   The Sausage Man)

Start this in two fry pans.

Core and seed peppers and slice onion.
In heated olive oil, start to fry.
In other fry pan, cut sausage into links and begin to cook.

Peppers will cook faster, so when done, just set aside until sausage is cooked.
Once sausage is cooked, add peppers and onions to pan to heat, and then you
are ready to make sandwiches.

Another way to change this dish is to add a can of Hunt's tomato sauce after
cooking. And now you have sausage & peppers in red gravy (sauce).

Either way, this is a great classic Italian sandwich.

Serve hot or cold.

FRIED CHICKEN CUTLETS

INGREDIENTS

1 pound chicken cutlets, trimmed
    and flattened

For the egg wash
1 cup flour
1 cup seasoned bread crumbs (add
    extra Parmigianino / Pecorino
    Romano cheese)
2 – 4 large eggs, beaten

Work on a sheet of wax paper with three bowls.

Dip the chicken cutlet, first in the egg, then flour, egg again, and then into the breadcrumbs.

Let this dry on the wax paper for about 10 to 15 minutes.

In deep skillet on medium heat, using vegetable oil, heat until oil is hot. Add one chicken cutlet at a time to pan, as many as the pan can hold. Cook, turning once, until golden brown.

Transfer the cutlets to a plate lined with paper towels to drain.

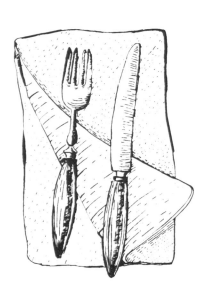

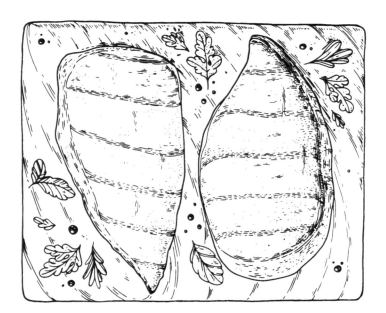

SAUSAGE STUFFED GARLIC BREAD

INGREDIENTS

1 large loaf French or Italian bread

12 tablespoons unsalted butter, softened

2 tablespoons olive oil

½ cup grated Parmesan cheese

1 ½ teaspoons Italian seasoning (preferably M.O.B. Seasoning)

2 teaspoons minced garlic

1 tablespoon finely chopped parsley

¼ teaspoon salt

1 tablespoon olive oil

¾ pound fresh sweet or hot Italian sausage, removed from casing

1 cup thinly sliced onion

½ cup thinly sliced green bell pepper or red pepper (or mix both)

Pinch of red pepper

1 tablespoon chopped garlic

Preheat oven to 375 degrees and line a large baking sheet with aluminum foil. Using a serrated knife, cut the bread lengthwise. Lay the two halves of bread cut-side-up on the lined baking sheet.

In a small mixing bowl, combine the butter, olive oil, grated parmesan, Italian seasoning, garlic, parsley, and salt, and mix well. Spread the butter mixture evenly on to the two halves of bread. Place on baking sheet and bake until just starting to get bubbly, but not brown (about 10 minutes). Remove from the oven.

Meanwhile in large skillet, heat the oil over medium heat. Add the sausage and cook, stirring and breaking up with a large wooden spoon, until cooked through and the fat is rendered. Remove with a slotted spoon and drain on a paper towel.

Add the onions, peppers, and sliced peppers. Cook, stirring until soft, about 5 minutes. Add garlic and cook another minute.

Remove from heat, add the sausage back to pan, and stir well. Spread the sausage and pepper mixture evenly over the bottom half of the bread and cover with the top half. Wrap in aluminum foil and return to oven to warm and for the flavors to blend, about 6 to 10 minutes. Remove from oven, keep wrapped until ready to slice, and serve.

M.O.B. SEASONING
(My Own Blend)

INGREDIENTS

1 tablespoon dried leaf oregano
1 tablespoon dried thyme
1 teaspoon dried basil
2 tablespoons garlic powder
1 tablespoon black pepper
2 ½ tablespoons paprika
1 tablespoon red hot pepper flakes

IN ALBINA'S PANTRY, there were always Mason jars with her mix of seasonings, dried parsley, dried basil, and anything else she had in her garden. Instead of buying seasonings, she made her own. She pretty much used this on everything.

Combine all ingredients thoroughly and store in Mason jar or an airtight container.

PASTA E FAGIOLI
(aka: Pasta and Bean)
(aka: Pasta Fazool)

INTERESTING NOTE ABOUT the name of this dish which has its own alias: I learned the proper spelling and pronunciation for this recipe. In my house, it was always called Pasta Fazool! But the proper pronunciation is Pasta e Fagioli (the "G" sounds like a "J"), and you need to pinch together your thumb with your index, middle, and ring fingers, and holding your hand just a little below your chin, move your hand front to back from your wrist as you say it. Just from this motion, BeBe knew what dish she would be making. And another side note. Dean Martin said it best in his rendition of "That's Amore," when they were trying to rhyme the word drool—"When the stars make you drool just like Pasta Fazool—That's Amore!!"

Grandpa

Pasta e Fagioli

INGREDIENTS

2 cans cannellini beans or small
white beans (use everything in
the can, including bean sludge,
for flavor)
1 28 ounce can San Marzano
tomatoes
½ can kitchen ready tomatoes
5 – 6 garlic cloves, diced or chopped
1 large Vidalia onion, chopped
Enough olive oil to cover the
bottom of a 6 or 8 quart pot
1 lb ditallini or elbow macaroni

Bring a pot of water to boil for the pasta.

Take your 6 – 8 quart pot, and drizzle in just enough olive oil to cover the bottom. Dice or chop the garlic, onion, and celery, and sauté in the olive oil until golden. Pour in the entire can of beans (do not drain) and the whole can of San Marzano tomatoes, breaking them up with your hands as you add them to the pot. Add ½ can of kitchen ready tomatoes. Add salt and pepper to taste. Bring to a boil, then reduce flame to a simmer.

Cook the pasta in a separate pot for 10 – 12 minutes. When the pasta is cooked, remove half of the water and set aside. Pour the contents of the bean mixture into the pasta and remaining water. Stir, and add some of the removed pasta water back in if the pasta e fagioli seems too thick.

Now this is ready to serve! Serve with nice garlic bread, a little drizzle of olive oil, and fresh grated Pecorino Romano cheese.

This will be a hit! And they will be back for more! Now, who doesn't want to be Italian?!

SUNDAY GRAVY

Albina

HAVE YOU EVER given up a long-held family tradition? Most of us along the way have. Times change, we don't have enough time, work, life is going too fast...

Like in many Italian-American families, my mother made gravy—a rich, tomato-based sauce with numerous cuts of meat—every Sunday. It was almost always served with macaroni (pasta), eggplant, chicken cutlets, and many other dishes, and we ritually ate every Sunday around 2:00pm. It wasn't until I was an adult that I realized how time consuming it was to make this enormous meal each week. My mom would start cooking at 7:00am, first seasoning the meat for the meatballs and then chopping the onions, parsley, and garlic. All this was done before she left for the 9:00am church service and I was instructed to stir the gravy. Most Sundays my breakfast was a freshly cooked meatball.

I'll admit, my love for Sunday Gravy faded over time as I became an adult, and with work and my own family, it seemed to go away. After my mom's passing and also the passing of many of my aunts and uncles, I would reminisce often about all of their cooking and those Sunday meals.

We seem so intent to remove ourselves from our culture that we grew up on. So on those days, longing for the connection to our Italian-American custom, I make Sunday Gravy!

It has been passed down and tweaked through the generations, but just the smell of gravy on the stove brings you right back to being a child again. I think the main reason so many give up on Sunday Gravy is that we are too culturally removed—not only from Italy, but from the even closer Rhode Island, Silver Lake, Federal Hill, Knightsville, and North Providence, RI areas and the traditions of our mothers and fathers childhoods and the large families we all came from.

Although I would love to share this recipe, I have been told that it is a family secret so it's off limits for publication. However, the statute of limitations has passed in reference to the family, and since BeBe is not with us anymore, I hope you enjoy the stories and reconnect to your family roots.

Start bringing back Sunday Gravy!!!

This next recipe was a little challenging since I have never followed instructions for Sunday Gravy.

In any Italian kitchen, this is made with passion so you can follow all the ingredients, but to get the true meaning of this recipe, you have to add the passion!

Sunday Gravy

INGREDIENTS

For the sauce

2 tablespoons olive oil

1 pound pork spare ribs or 2 thick
    pork chops

1 pound Italian sausage (I use sweet
    sausage but hot is good also)

4 cloves garlic

1 small onion

1 small can tomato paste

3 28 or 35 ounce cans Italian toma-
    toes, crushed or kitchen ready
    chunky style (I suggest San Mar-
    zano or Pastene brand)

1 can water (2 cups)

Salt & pepper

Parsley and basil leaves, chopped
    (or if dried 1 to 2 teaspoons)

In fry pan, brown the pork and Italian sausage in olive oil. I add a little red table wine (optional). When done browning, remove the meat from the pan and use this oil to start the sauce.

In a large heavy pot over medium heat, add the oil from the fry pan.
Add the garlic and chopped onion to cook for about 2 to 5 minutes.
Add the pork and the sausage to pan.

Add ½ cup of red table wine at this time. This is optional.
Now add the cans of tomato and a can of water to the pan.

At this time add salt and pepper, parsley, and basil.
Now add the tomato paste.
Add 1 tablespoon of sugar (this is also optional).
Bring the sauce to a simmer, partially covering the pot and cook over low heat, stirring occasionally for at least 2 hours.
If the sauce becomes too thick, add a little more water.

ITALIAN MEATBALLS

INGREDIENTS

2 lbs ground beef *or* a combination of:
    1 lb ground beef
    ½ lb ground veal
    ½ lb ground pork
1 loaf Italian bread; tear out the
    inside and soak in milk
1 cup Italian seasoned breadcrumbs
2 large eggs
2 cloves garlic, minced
1 small onion, chopped
3 tablespoons finely chopped flat-
    leaf parsley (or dried parsley)
½ cup Pecorino Romano or Parmi-
    giano-Reggiano cheese, or a mix
    of the two
1 teaspoon salt
Freshly ground pepper

Combine all the ingredients in a large bowl.
Mix together thoroughly.

I mix with my hands to feel the texture.
If too loose, add a little more breadcrumbs.
If too dry, add 1 more egg or a little olive oil.

Drizzle olive in your hands and start to shape and roll the meatballs.

Two options to cook:

Oven method
Heat oven to 350 degrees.
Line cookie sheet with parchment paper.
Roll meatballs, place on cookie sheet, drizzle with olive oil and bake approximately 20 minutes, turning meatballs over after first ten minutes.
These will finish cooking when you place them in the sauce.

Stovetop method
In fry pan, heat olive oil.
Add the meatballs and brown them well on all sides.
Transfer the meatballs to a plate.
Add to sauce.

ALBINA'S CHICKEN ESCAROLE SOUP

INGREDIENTS

2 whole chicken breasts, bone in

1 ½ gallon water in a large stockpot

4 good quality chicken bouillon
 cubes (Knorr or Minor)

2 good quality beef bouillon cubes
 (Knorr or Minor)

1 large Spanish or sweet onion, left
 whole, but peeled

6 large celery ribs, diced

1 (8 ounce) can of whole or diced
 tomatoes

2 heads of fresh escarole

½ pound – 1 pound soup pasta
 (any kind is fine)

Salt & pepper to taste

First wash the escarole very well. Escarole can be very sandy, so take the time to wash it thoroughly. Then blanch the escarole in a separate pot of water until tender, strain, rinse with cold water, squeeze all the extra water out, and set aside. Put the large stockpot on the stove with all the vegetables, canned tomato, and bouillon. When the stock comes to a boil, add the chicken and boil until cooked (15 minutes), then remove chicken and set aside until it cools enough to handle. Meanwhile, allow the stock to continue simmering. Chop the escarole, debone and chop the chicken. Add back the chicken and escarole. Allow to simmer on stove. In a separate pot, boil the soup pasta. Remove the whole onion and discard. Taste and adjust the seasoning with salt and pepper. Add soup pasta and enjoy!

SPAGHETTI AGLIO E OLIO
(Garlic and Oil)

INGREDIENTS

1 pound spaghetti

4 garlic cloves, finely chopped

½ cup plus 1 tablespoon extra-virgin olive oil

¾ teaspoon crushed red pepper flakes

3 tablespoons chopped flat-leaf parsley

6 – 10 anchovy filets / black olives (optional)

Place garlic and oil in a cold pan and cook over medium heat until the garlic has sizzled for a minute but not colored. This is when you would add the anchovies and black olives. It is best to start this just a minute or two before your pasta is cooked.

Add the red pepper flakes to the pan, then add the drained pasta also with about 6 tablespoons of the pasta cooking water. Sauté together for a few seconds, toss in the parsley, and serve.

PASTA WITH PARMESAN CHEESE & BUTTER

INGREDIENTS

1 box (pound) of your favorite pasta
8 tablespoons unsalted butter
½ cup fresh grated Parmesan cheese
½ teaspoon fresh cracked pepper

ALBINA MADE THIS for us when we were kids and we loved it! Looking for that quick and delicious dinner? This will do.

Prepare the pasta according to the directions on the box. While pasta is cooking, melt butter in a large skillet. Drain pasta when done and add to the melted butter in the skillet. Toss to coat.

Now transfer to serving bowl, toss in the Parmesan cheese and black pepper, and enjoy!

CRACKED SICILIAN OLIVES

INGREDIENTS

Sicilian olives (pitted—no pits)
Fresh-sliced thin celery
Diced garlic
Diced carrots
Lemon zest
Chopped Italian parsley
Italian spices
Olive oil
Red wine vinegar

Mix all together in bowl. Store in refrigerator. (My mom always used Mason jars.) Serve with nice crusty garlic bread!

BAMBI'S DRINK

It's raining, it's pouring, Bambi is snoring.

BAMBINO IS MY dad. When he was born, my grandmother Laura's English was not too good. They handed her the baby, and when they asked her what his name is, she just responded, "My *bambino*," (baby boy) and that is how he got his name. Bambi became a construction worker. Back in the day, when it would rain, there was no work for Bambi. This of course was a problem since Bambi didn't know about Albina's cooking job.

So, on these days, I would see the car pull up, BeBe would look out of the second floor window and would wave them away. "You have the wrong house," she would yell out and the car would pull away. All this while Bambi was snoring.

On these days, BeBe cooked for Bambi. She made the best egg dishes and would serve Bambi his favorite coffee drink, which she called a coffee eggnog.

Bambi

INGREDIENTS

1 cup of very strong brewed coffee, hot

1 egg

Cream

Dash of vanilla

In small bowl, crack one egg and whisk until it starts to froth.
In coffee cup, add cream, dash of vanilla, and whisked egg.

EGGS IN TOMATO

INGREDIENTS

1 garlic clove, crushed
2 tablespoons olive oil
2 cups canned tomato puree
4 fresh basil leaves, torn into pieces
Salt and pepper
Pinch of sugar
8 large eggs
Freshly grated Parmigiano-Reggiano
    or Pecorino Romano cheese

In medium skillet, simmer garlic in oil over medium heat.
Add tomato puree, basil, salt, pepper, and sugar.
Bring to a simmer and cook for about 15 minutes, or until sauce is thickened.

Break an egg into a small cup. With a spoon, make a well in the tomato sauce.
Slide the egg into the sauce.
Continue with the remaining eggs. Sprinkle with cheese.
Cover and cook for approximately 3 minutes or until the eggs are done.
Serve with Italian toast.

ALBINA'S WINE BISCUITS

INGREDIENTS

4 to 4 ½ cups of flour

3 teaspoons Rumford Baking
  Powder

Pinch of salt

1 cup of vegetable or canola oil

1 cup of red wine (Carlo Rossi
  preferred)

1 cup of sugar

1 egg, beaten

Make a well with the flour, baking powder, and salt. Add in the oil, wine, and sugar. Mix with a spoon then knead with your hands. Work into a soft texture. You don't want the dough to be sticky or too dry. Add a little water with oil or more wine if too dry; more flour if too sticky.

Roll out long ropes of dough and cut each to make a bite-size circle until all the dough is on cookie sheets. Brush each with the beaten egg.
Bake at 350 degrees until they get brown. Approximate 14 to 18 minutes.

Can also use white wine for a different flavor. If having trouble rolling dough, simply make bite-size wine nuggets! Either way, these biscuits are delicious!

LEMON EGG BISCUITS

INGREDIENTS

Biscuits
6 cups of flour

1 ½ cups of sugar

3 tablespoons of baking powder

6 eggs

2 tablespoons of lemon extract or
vanilla

1 cup of oil (Crisco oil)

½ cup of milk (whole milk)

Lemon glaze
1 box of confectioners sugar

1 tablespoon of lemon extract

4 tablespoons of milk (more if
needed)

Mix all of these ingredients in order and form dough. Roll into small balls. Place on cookie sheet and bake at 350 degrees for approximate 15 minutes.

Mix the lemon glaze ingredients together and dip top of cookies in. Add sprinkles.

RICOTTA-PINEAPPLE PIE

If ever you need a favor, this is the pie to bring—make them a pie they can't refuse.

INGREDIENTS

A 9 inch pie pan or springform pan

1 tablespoon unsalted butter,
    softened
1/4 cup graham cracker crumbs
1/2 cup sugar
2 tablespoons cornstarch
1 15-ounce container ricotta cheese
2 large eggs
1/2 cup heavy cream
1 teaspoon grated lemon zest
1 teaspoon vanilla extract

Topping
1 20-ounce can crushed pineapple
    in syrup
1/4 cup sugar
1 tablespoon cornstarch
2 tablespoons lemon juice

Preheat oven to 350°F.

Spread the butter over the bottom and sides of pan. Add the crumbs, turning pan to coat the bottom and sides. In large bowl, stir together the sugar and cornstarch. Add the ricotta, eggs, cream, lemon zest, and vanilla and beat until smooth. Pour mixture into prepared pan. Bake for 50 minutes, or until pie is set around the edges but the center is slightly soft. Cool to room temperature on a wire rack.

TOPPING
Drain the pineapple well in strainer, reserving 1/2 cup of liquid. In a medium saucepan, stir together the sugar and cornstarch. Stir in the 1/2 cup pineapple juice and the lemon juice. Cook, stirring, until thickened, about 1 minute. Add the pineapple. Remove from heat and let cool. Spread the pineapple mixture over the pie.

Chill for at least 1 hour before serving.

COOKING AND CLEANLINESS RULES
FOR SANITARY COOKING AND EATING

THEY SAY THAT cleanliness is next to godliness. It is also elbow-to-elbow with the healthiness, and therefore a responsibility of each and all.

Growing up in Rhode Island, we never went to a restaurant where we didn't know the owner(s), chef, kitchen staff, wait staff, or bartender. We didn't need a health rating displayed on the door; we just knew the places were safe.

Always, *always* wash your hands before and after eating, especially after shaking hands. And forget about it if you visited someone in the hospital! Hospitals are where we can get sick, where there are germs... don't only wash your hands—change and wash the clothes you had on as well.

Regarding leftovers—eat within 24 hours. I know we all *intend* eat that chicken parm and spaghetti that we took home, or that half Italian grinder sitting in the fridge. Just remember that gabagool that's been sitting in there for a week could end send you on a trip to the ER, and that's where germs meet... and mingle.

TIPS FROM MY KITCHEN TO YOURS

I HAVE BEEN known to be a Kitchen Diva. I manage my kitchen as if it were a 5-star restaurant. Every dish I create and serve is done with care. I also use food handling gloves, always wear an apron, use marpinas, and use plenty of paper towels.

I see these cooks on these very famous cooking shows—no aprons or gloves and their hair isn't even pulled back! Not in my kitchen. Even if you are cooking with me, gloves are always worn when it comes to food handling.

To keep things simple and have dishes that are easy to prepare, you have to start with well-stocked shelves.

It kind of defeats the purpose if you have to stop at the market every night to get ingredients to make even a simple meal. So try to maintain some main ingredients to have on hand to make cooking and preparing meals more enjoyable, rather than just a task.

KITCHEN PANTRY / CLOSET
Pasta / Rice
Canned beans
Canned tomatoes
Tomato paste
Chicken broth
Italian Seasoned Bread Crumbs
Panko bread crumbs

REFRIGERATOR
Unsalted butter
Milk
Large eggs
Cream cheese
Romano / Parmesan cheese
Vidalia or yellow onions
Garlic
Bagged mixed greens
Carrots
Celery
Lemons

FREEZER
Ground beef
Boneless skinless chicken breast
    and thighs
Hot or sweet Italian sausage
Gelato (any flavor)
Ice cream (any flavor)

It was well into my adulthood before I realized I was an American. For most second-generation Italian-American children who grew up in the 40's, 50's, 60's, and 70's, there was a definite distinction between us and Americans. We were Italians. Everybody else, they were Americans. I was born American and lived here all my life, but "Americans" were people who ate peanut butter and jelly sandwiches on mushy white bread. I had no animosity toward them, it's just I thought ours was the better way, with our bread man, egg man, vegetable man, and chicken man, just to name a few of the peddlers who came to our neighborhoods. We knew and them they knew us.

My grandfather, Pasquale, lived on the first floor of my mother's three-family house. I felt so connected to him. He shared many stories with me and we spoke Italian. When my grandfather died, things began to change. My mother no longer spoke Italian in the house.

My grandparents were Italian-Italians, my parents were Italian-Americans. I'm an American-Italian. Call it culture, call it roots, I still feel very much Italian and feel blessed that I experienced such a wonderful piece of my heritage. This is what I bring to the dishes that I cook and prepare for my family, extended family, nieces, nephews, and friends!

CPSIA information can be obtained
at www.ICGtesting.com
Printed in the USA
BVRC102246301121
622875BV00003B/58